FALLING FOR A DOLPHIN

P9-CAM-083

FALLING
FOR A
DOLPHIN

Heathcote Williams

Arcade Publishing · New York
Little, Brown and Company

COPYRIGHT © 1990 BY HEATHCOTE WILLIAMS

ALL RIGHTS RESERVED. NO PART OF THIS BOOK MAY BE REPRODUCED IN
ANY FORM OR BY ANY ELECTRONIC OR MECHANICAL MEANS, INCLUDING
INFORMATION STORAGE AND RETRIEVAL SYSTEMS, WITHOUT PERMISSION
IN WRITING FROM THE PUBLISHER, EXCEPT BY A REVIEWER WHO MAY
QUOTE BRIEF PASSAGES IN A REVIEW.

FIRST U.S. EDITION 1991

ISBN 1-55970-114-5
Library of Congress Catalog Card Number 90-55445
Library of Congress Cataloging-in-Publication information is
available.

Published in the United States by Arcade Publishing, Inc.,
New York, a Little, Brown company

10 9 8 7 6 5 4 3 2 1

PRINTED IN ITALY

It is an important and popular fact that things are not always what they seem. For instance, on the planet Earth, man had always assumed that he was more intelligent than dolphins because he had achieved so much – the wheel, New York, wars and so on – whilst all the dolphins had ever done was muck about in the water having a good time. But conversely, the dolphins had always believed that they were far more intelligent than man – for precisely the same reasons.

Douglas Adams,
The Hitchhiker's Guide to the Galaxy

'Is there anything else I need . . . ?'

A wet-suit lies on the diving-shop floor:
An undulating mass of black and red blubber.
Beside it, a bag of industrial polythene,
Filled with breathing-tubes, weights and weight-belt;
Palm-shaped flippers, and a mask.

'No,' says the proprietor,
'Just add water. To taste.'

Daingean Uí Chúis.
The Eask Peninsula.
At the edge of the Atlantic.
Dawn.

Outcrops of metamorphic rock,
Crumpled sheets and rippling curtains of mud,
Slowly tilted upright and petrified.
Great grey escarpments, tipped with blanket bog.

The turf-topped ruins of bee-hive houses,
From the Stone Age,
Dot the landscape, like blunt canines.

Disused cornfields crumble into the sea . . .
Clumps of thrift.
Only the faintest ghosts of tillage.

Round ziggurats of stone,
Washed down by the tides
Into splintered spirals
Like Towers of Babel
And layered with seams of illusory Kerry diamonds,
Loom out of the sea.

A set built a hundred and seventy million years
Before the birth of the Himalayas;
Inaccessible from land.

The caves, made from collapsed leaves of *millefeuille* rock,
Echo with the conversation of guillemots,
Wheatears, choughs, and gannets.

Sea-crows, large as umbrellas,
Take an unhurried view of any outside visit.

A turnstone pecks silently at barnacles.
Foam hisses through cracks in a reef.

The only mammal for miles is rumoured to live here.
A hermit dolphin.
Quietly fishing for pollock, wrasse and conger;
Occasionally diverted by fishermen:
Riding their bow-waves,
Treating their boats as ambulatory Jacuzzi,
Racing and overtaking ninety-horsepower engines;
Then shooting towards the pale blue mountains
Of Macgillycuddy's Reeks . . .
Vanishing in search of some more testing sport.

The lighthouse keeper, Paddy Ferriter,
Sighted it four years ago;

Then a local fisherman, Lawrence Benison,
Passed on the changing details of its solitary haunts.

This I-Spy genealogy led to an invitation:
'You must come.'

A week later, the wet-suit,
Inhabited,
Lies spread-eagled on the surface of the water.

Mauve jellyfish drift past,
Blinking their whole bodies.

Like them, you move only with the wind and the tide,
Nature's public transport.
The individual will is put on hold.

Fronds of kelp and dulse, strapped to the bottom,
Surge and thrash below you,
Caught in submarine storms
That feature in no weather report.

You waft in random directions:
First towards the Inch, then Crow Rock,
Then Doulus Head, and then the Blasket Islands.

You flick your fingers noiselessly underwater,
As instructed.
You tap the metal weights upon your belt
Repeatedly with a pebble
Clutched in the cold fingers of one hand.

There is no sign of it.

You remind yourself that the creature,
Somewhere in this chilling expanse of water,
Is wild, and not a dog or a cottage cat
To be manipulated.

It can detect you from five miles distant,
Make up its own mind whether or not to appear...
And there may be more of its mind
To be made up.

There is still no sign of it.

Adrift in the sea,
In a mild state of sensory deprivation,
Your inner voice becomes more audible:
Demanding to know, from time to time,
What on earth it is that you think you are doing.

You swim a few masterful strokes, in response,
While being blown about, uncontrollably,
As directionless as a piece of litter.

The Atlantic currents have quickly taken you
Half a mile from shore.

The inner voice persists.
You reply to it by thinking that you are no longer quite on the
    earth,
Where that inner voice has hatched its authority,
But are suspended between one world and another –
A place where you have no bearings –
Like a hang-glider lost in unmapped continents of clouds.

Voices from the night before
Now make themselves heard with added impact:
Warnings of compass-point jellyfish,
Lethal as curare,
With thin, spidery tentacles,
Inducing coma, then drowning . . .

Porbeagle sharks, brought in by a warm spell,
Surface swimmers, nine feet long . . .

The pebble takes on more significance:
Your grip on this acoustic distress-flare tightens,
It is pathetically tapped with greater frequency.
To no effect.

The Atlantic rollers flick at you
Like school bullies
Remorselessly tormenting some hapless victim with wet towels,
And reminding you that death lives very locally.
About six inches away.

Then you remember the last voice of the night before:
'. . . Just call its name.'
'Its name . . . ?'
'It has a load of names . . . '
He shrugged.
'We just call it the dolphin.
You call out "dolphin" and it comes.'

You call, repeatedly,
Shouting the word into the salty gusts of wind
Sweeping into your face,
Then absurdly diving beneath the surface to escape a driving
   shower;
To see again if there is any sign of it below.

There is none.

Slowly you forget about it,
And forget the dangers, so teasingly described,
As you drift across the surface,
Half-hypnotised.

A scrap of your old, reptile brain
Freshly reminds you
That you came from the sea;
That you are composed mainly of water;
That the minerals in the ocean
Are present in your bloodstream
In the same proportions,
Sodium, potassium, chlorine . . .
And so, being here,
Unwillingly bent double,
Mauled by Atlantic swells,
Up-ended by the undertow
Is not wholly incongruous.

A fleck of flesh,
Coated in rubber;
Once on land,
Now back in the water;

And peering down at a translucent underworld
In an atavistic trance.

As lumpy tussocks of water smash together
You are ionised by the charge,
Contact drunk on the sea.
Every drop of it descended
From cometary ice.

The water, to which you owe your life,
First came to the planet
As a rain of icy comets,
Which then dissolved,
Vaporising on impact with the earth's aurora.

. . .You peer down
At minute ancestors,
Moving with ease through three dimensions
As if still in the space they came from.

You gaze at the delicate life forms that begat you:
Developing just beneath the surface
To seal themselves off from harmful ultraviolet light.

You float along the ceiling of another kingdom,
Where gravity is suspended,
Looking down into the vague regions of your past.

Silica dust quivers constantly,
Shimmering through the water
Like the clouds of multi-coloured phosphenes
That gather together within your closed eyelids
Before you fall asleep.

Suddenly, your blood undergoes a sea-change.
Your body jerks, shuddering like a rocket on take-off:
Half in the air, half still in ground effect.
The rumoured creature lies beside you in the water.

A bare hint of movement in its tail,
Then quite still.

Eye to eye.

Twelve, fifteen feet long.
Half a ton in weight.
Sleek, and silvery as the moon.

It has approached you, indetectably, from behind.
You suppress an impulse to spin round hastily:
Anxious to see from where, exactly, this apparition came,
Fearing you would take in water through the tube,
And drown.

It draws closer,
Setting no wash.
Staring.
Its grey, telling eye
Inches from yours.

You stare back, startled,
Caught off guard by an intelligence
Both knowing and remote.

With a single movement
It disappears,
As if to allow you to digest the visitation.

When the involuntary spurts of adrenalin
Discharged into the surrounding water
Are diluted,
And the shock-waves have ebbed,

It returns
To move up and down your body,
Spraying each section of it with a barrage of echo-locating
    clicks:
Penetrating your brain, heart, lungs, stomach, groin, legs and
    feet;
Seeming to gauge each in depth . . .
Mapping your body's geography
In punctilious detail.

Your brain tingles oddly
As it is spattered, in a second examination,
With unfathomable waves of sound and ultra-sound.

The dolphin then rises to the surface,
Releasing a deep gust of air from the top of its domed head,

And inhales beside you,
The unexpected sound of breathing,
In isolation, in the ocean,
Creating an arresting affinity.

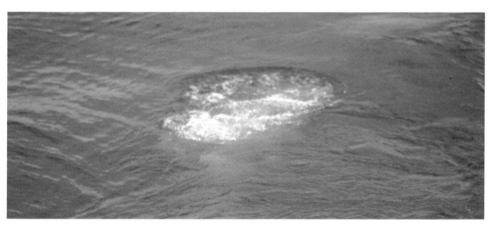

The valve in its blow-hole closes –
A faint chink of cartilage.

Two air-breathing mammals
Side by side:

One blinkered, uncoordinated
And cluttered with plastic accessories;

The other in careless control,
A wide-eyed virtuoso,
Master of a larger territory than yours
And, unlike other animals,
Unnervingly disinclined to be outstared.

Your skin prickles,
Physically registering the dolphin's prodigious strength;
Quickening you to the fact that one dissembling move –
The betrayal of even one false thought, you're prone to feel –
And it could stave in your body
With a lackadaisical flick of its fin;

Torpedo into you at thirty knots,
Snapping your spine as if it were a sardine's;
Crush each limb into fragments with its jaws,
And eighty-eight needle-sharp, conical teeth.

But it appears to entertain no such wish.
And all such apprehensions are swiftly dissolved
By its expression:
A three-foot smile,
A tender-lipped antidote to panic.

Its face is permanently engraved with this subtle, potent smile,
As if a smile were the only facial gesture worth making,
And it had therefore settled into a genetic trait:
The emblem of its seductive ability
To disarm a fellow-creature –
Whom it should have been persuaded
Was its most intractable enemy –
By the only safe method: making friends.

Close to,
The benign fixture becomes more complex:
The smile flickers from a droll interest,
Through bemused pity

To a wry, patrician glance of transcendence.

The dolphin's presence in the water –
Electrically alive to each goggle-eyed gaze,
Each hampered, blundering movement in the water –
Poultices out embarrassed gurgles, by way of greeting.

Despite yourself, you are compelled to speak,
To blurt out a succession of stilted, staccato phrases through
    the breathing-tube:
' . . . Hello,'
And, 'I'm pleased to meet you . . . '
Each one more prostratedly foolish than the last.
And each one barely intelligible
Even to your own ears,
Spluttered through water,
Its little sense buried by burbling gasps.

The dolphin whistles, then clicks, rhythmically,
Then makes a sound like the creaking of a door,
A rusty hinge. It whistles again.
There's a rattle, resembling a chuckle.

You try to guess the meaning from its tone,
Like a tongue-tied foreigner,
Desperately striving to understand the hermetic kernel of a
    language,
The sure clue to consciousness.

It speaks again.
You make some spontaneous noises in reply,
Less inhibited.

The dolphin draws closer,
Gently nudging your mask with its upper lip
To expose your face.

It touches your cheek,
Nuzzling your skin,
Then moves away
With a glance that seems to invite you
To stroll, horizontally, in a direction of its choosing.

You accept.
Magnetically allured by a very complete stranger.
Willingly locked into its company.

You tentatively reach out
To stroke its smooth, unscaled skin.
Soft as a child's flesh,
As you waft silently in the dolphin's company
Past the Foze Rock, the Tailor's Iron,
The Sorrowful Cliffs,
And a reef called the Bank of the Gardens of the Mouth.

Marooned beside a living raft,
And understanding how sea-creatures of the past
Were reputed to beguile sailors,
Persuading them that they were entering a well of
    forgetfulness –
Unaware that in the sharp bliss of that sea-creature's song
Centuries were passing.

The distant landmass loses its pull.

You swim together,
Enmeshed in a febrile elation;

Running away to sea.

Your lungs, two portable sacs of air –
Eight pints, now treasured instead of being taken for granted –
Are spun out like emergency rations
As you descend
To greet it below.

It disappears in a puff of spray,

Then reappears so quickly on the horizon
You think it must have a companion . . .

It plunges, lost to view.

You wait.
Lost now without it.
Five minutes . . . ten . . .
Vulnerable. A little afraid.

A dark fin surfaces, fifty yards away. . .
Your inner voice, still auditioning,
Whispers, 'Shark.'
It has whispered the word constantly
As you peered at every fin-shaped wave,
Relieved when the tense tip broke and spilt.

The dark fin approaches,
The frisson, induced by the uncertain silhouette,
Serving to remind you of the received wisdom of your tribe –
On the off-chance you had been tempted
To hurl it overboard.

The dark fin draws closer still.

Your reason tells you that the sharks here
Are filter-feeders, harmless, even a threatened species;
There'd be a million to one chance against meeting a Blue
    shark,
An occasional summer migrant.
But your reason is unceremoniously drowned in sweat.

The dark fin is beside you

. . . The dolphin's fin,
Shaped like a thorn on a rose.

It has found its way to you
With the accuracy of a bat
Beaming in on a moth.

An hour goes by.
Side by side with someone as strange
As a mixture of a Martian and a mermaid,
In alien territory.

Its rounded, orb-like head
Containing a brain

The size of yours
And half as big again.

An intelligence nurtured in the sea:
One that has arisen quite unassisted
By the surfeit of stimuli
The human intelligence has concocted
To gorge itself upon.

Its foetal features
Compelling you to wonder with what plot
Evolution may decide to favour it.

There's a distant splash.
You look up and see a long, mottled fish,
Flashing and spinning vertically above the water,
Its scales coruscating in the sun, like mica.

It's being hurled up vigorously from below,
Fifteen, twenty feet,
Then it falls, smacking the surface;
Three times,
Then silence.

You scrutinise the ripples,
And vainly scan the surface of the water.
Then your hand is brushed insistently from below
By the tail of a black pollock
Held in the dolphin's mouth.

You lower your head into the water.
It is presented to you.
Its flesh unblemished, drowned by air.
Vitamin-fresh *sushi*.

Stunned, you attempt a token bite,
And then return it, to be swallowed in one clean suck.

You meet the dolphin's stare,
The sense of some old alliance rekindled.

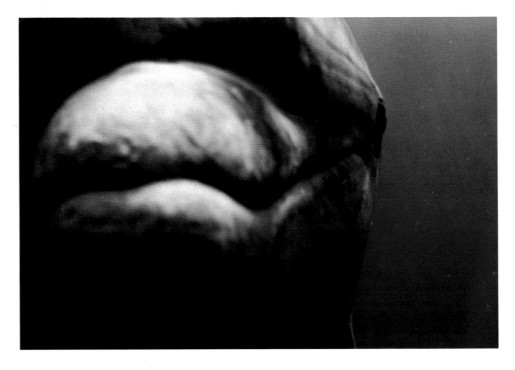

And you brood upon the truth of the old wives' tale
Of fish being good for the brain,
The lipids and protein in fish
Now revealed to have a similar structure to cerebral tissue –
And fish is a diet you both have in common.

It vanishes again, inexplicably,
Through the jade-green mist,

To digest the pollock . . . ? to sleep . . . ?
To fish again . . . ? to drift in thought . . . ?
Then, like lightning, reappears,
Uncannily choosing the moment
When you are thinking of it
Most intently.

And you become easily, euphorically persuaded
By this large, eerie and susceptive presence
That you are exchanging particles of thought,
Mutually mixing some telepathic cocktail.

You know, instinctively, that there is some strange exchange,
And you become quite unconcerned
By the thought of shore-based familiars
Snorting with derision at the soft-headed crankiness of it,
For without this indefinable exchange
You would be drawing a blank,
Cutting the dolphin dead.

And your mind feels recharged by the nameless wildness of this
    creature,
So stretched that you effortlessly think of it as a person,
Of your two minds blending,
Your mind reaching out and becoming one with another.

And if bio-electricity travels beyond the cranium,
As it does,
And if a current travels faster through water,
With less resistance,
As it does,
Then who knows that a dolphin doesn't overhear what you're
    thinking.
When its elevated head lies in the water next to yours,
It's not hard to think that it does.

A mosaic of sound-waves,
Compressed, then rarefied, then compressed again,
Penetrates your mind.
First what seems like a mimicry
Of your own burbling in the water;
Then a stream of imitations
Sounding like trains, planes, car-horns –
Noises picked up from the shore, your habitat,
And relayed back to you,
Now estranged,
By way of reassurance.

The dolphin then reverts to its own language,
Flooding you with a barrage of pulsed tones.
You feel for a moment as if you have wandered into a
    subterranean cavern
Decorated with an arcane script,
And you can only continue in an obscure rite of passage
By deciphering it . . .

The sounds have an unsettling effect
As though coming from some huge bird impossibly flying
    underwater beside you,
Singing.

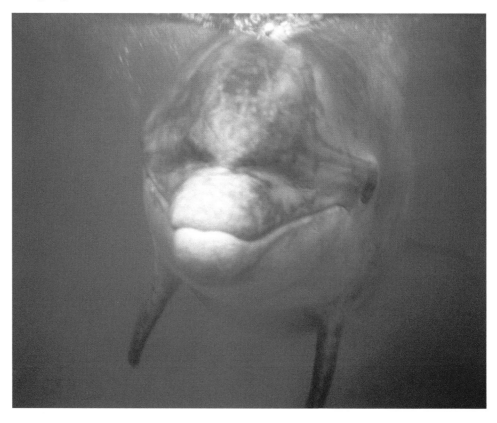

You are compelled to reply,
Without knowing what your reply is in response to.
And as you become caught up in this one-way conversation,
Out of your depth,
And as the invisible fibres of high frequency sounds pervade
    you,
They seem to be slyly skinning you of antique armouring,
Stressful inconsistencies.

Your grip on the little basket of human manias you clutch so
    firmly
Relaxes . . .
You begin to think how little there is to prevent you staying . . .
The cold . . . ?
Now overcome by this large, warm drop of flesh beside you.

The rush of abstract sound ebbs . . .
Was it just a series of conditioned signals,
Designed to stun a prey?
Even if it was only that . . .
It has succeeded.

The dolphin stares at you.
Its brain free-floating –
Spending none of its power
Contending with gravity.

When scientists scan the universe for intelligent life
Preference is given to those planets which are water-based.
The dolphin's elusive sapience prompts unaccustomed questions.

Who is to say that *you* are in sole charge of evolution . . . ?
That you are the be all and end all
Of this particular planet's experiment in self-awareness . . . ?
Only you.

The refreshing tribal treachery
Rouses thoughts of what might have been
Had your genes been pointing in another direction . . .
The past, differently handled,
Could have been the springboard
For a quite different present.

You are edged back into the shadows of some shared dream . . .
A surreptitious continuity, running parallel with yours,
And conveniently overlooked.

For what explains the curious sense of being greeted by the
    dolphin
As a long-lost friend . . . ?

Was it that once upon a time
You both grew up together –
The cave-dwelling human, living off crustaceans,
Anxious to form some compact with the dolphin,
A superior hunter whose skills you admired . . .
The dolphin, in its turn, intrigued by the dexterity of the
	human hand . . .

Is there a ghost of an ancestral treaty
For mutual survival,
As you shared
And share
This earth's fragile hospitality?

And what explains the sense of some ancient, hidden nature
Overlapping somewhere along the line with man's . . .
A nature venerated in antiquity,
When this shape-shifting sea-sprite
Was Poseidon's messenger, a Gaian pilot . . .
A demi-god.

All much less quirky, less sentimental
When you are inches away
Looking into its lake-like eye.

The dolphin surges up,
Its head above the water,
Then all of its body –
Tail-walking . . .
Walking on the water . . .

Is it in imitation of your dog-paddling stance, as it skitters with
   its tail;
Or mimicking upright mammals
Glimpsed on the distant shore-line, sauntering along the
   strand;
Or starting a new religion, a Delphic Christianity,
With a tossed-off acrobatic miracle,
Levitating half a ton with a flick of a fan . . . ?

It lowers itself slowly into the water,
Like Excalibur.
And then remains level with your body.
It seems to detect that you are flagging;
Shrouds you with one flipper,
Supports you with another,
Keeping you both afloat
With the eddying wake
From its muscular outboard below.

Your heads are together,
Your body grasped and scalloped by its smooth, flat arms
In what feels like an embrace.

You hear the appalled voice of a sceptic friend:
'But where do you think it will *lead* . . . ?
What can it *come* to . . . in the *end*?'

And, as in an unrestrained romance, you ignore the question,
Refusing to acknowledge the impossibility. . .

Again, as if in response to thought,
The dolphin breaks away,

Its arms spreading apart in an open gesture:
Supplication . . . ? benediction . . . ? a shrug . . . ?

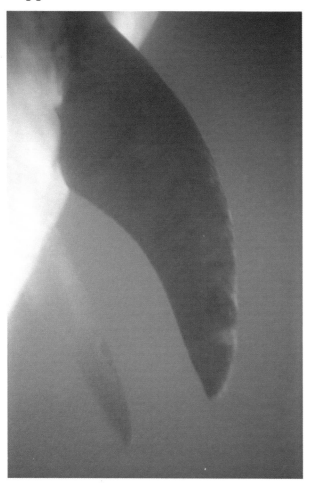

Its palms outwards, then quizzically turned
And dropped to its side.

You know you are reading too much into the gestures,
But you also know that they are not merely mechanical,
Performed for the benefit of some behaviourist's graph of
    trigger-signals and response.

And if you didn't read them,
You would be blinding yourself to the character of a creature
Who was making itself felt in the world
Long before you were thought of.

The dolphin descends,
Swimming around you, mercurially,
And you pursue it again below.
It whirls and coils,
Describing three-dimensional hieroglyphs in its watery space,
Then glances across at you.
A pencil-thin stream of bubbles pours from its blow-hole
As it speaks.
Again, you are lost for a reply,
Immersed in this its element,
Knowing less than nothing.

Above the entrance
Of the oracle of its namesake, Delphi,
Was written the salutary phrase *Gnothi seauton* – Know thyself.

And all you know
Is that its serene assurance
Suggests that it knows exactly how to be a dolphin,
And few humans have the foresight to be human.

You float back up.
It thrusts itself after you, bursting through the surface
And leaping through the air like a rainbow above your muddled
    head,

As if accounting it
And its billions of bemused neurons
No more significant than a bobbing buoy.

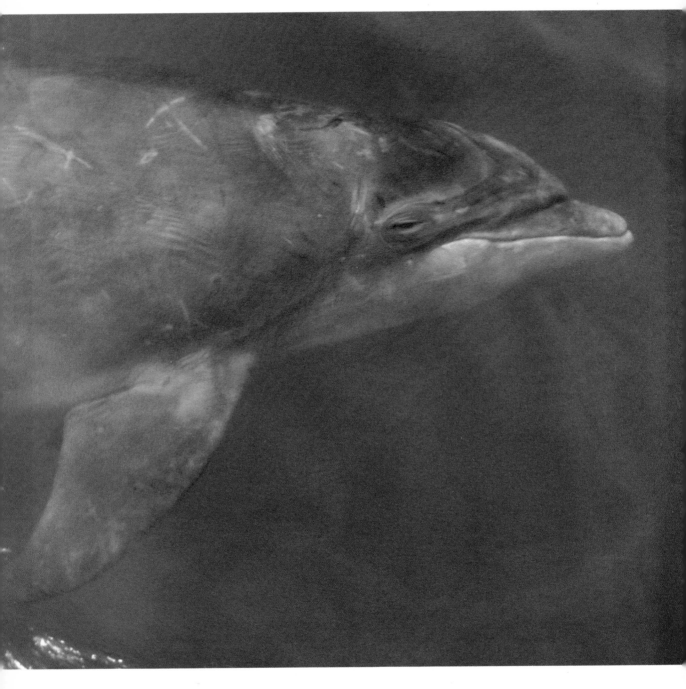

It plummets
Then rises again, circling you on the surface,
Fixing you with a look
That seems calculated to incinerate all further resistance.

It sidles down beneath your legs,
Parting them with its bottle-nose,
And slowly rises,
Deftly tuning itself to your centre of gravity.

As you find a handhold on its dorsal fin.

Its muscles tense. It bends its backbone,
Levering its flukes up and down,
And explodes into action,

Sculling and skimming across the water,
Rising and falling like a barrage balloon.

Ten, fifteen, twenty knots –
You gasp for breath
As you are scooped in and out of the water,

Trying to kneel, slipping,

A rickety human outrigger
Drawn through a tornado of foam,
Shouting ecstatic childish smatterings,
Swept along in a ferment of physicality,
Then buried in the water, then surfacing
And gasping and choking again

As the wind knocks the air back down your lungs
And breathing seems as hard
As drinking water from a fire-hydrant.

The dolphin draws to a halt.

You fall forward beside its blow-hole,
Inhaling its warm breath, as you come to rest
In a pool below the cliffs of Ballymacadoyle.

The dolphin lets you slip from its back,
Planting you near the safety of a rock.

You perch there, ecstatic, as the dolphin glides away,
Clinging to what has just occurred
And cautioning yourself that such feelings, clung to,
Swiftly turn to self-regard, and vanish like fairy gold.

. . . Had it thought that you were drowning?
Was the contact an interview

To assess your potential as a pet?
Or had it echo-located some knotted anxiety
Now released
As you let yourself get carried away. . . ?

You gaze at the dolphin,
Now carelessly fishing in the private crevices
Of the Eask Peninsula;
Slapping its tail down upon the surface
To change some subaquatic status quo.

As it dances into the distance,

And as you shiver, repeatedly,
At the bite of a south-easterly wind,
And watch it from the safety of dry land,
Now barrelling through a comfortless quilt of spitting waves,

Its life suddenly seems gruesomely austere.

And yet
It is lived out in places
Where a luminous beauty is its daily diet.

At every moment it absorbs the fugitive delicacy
Of its liquid underworld;
An aquanaut, sailing through a landscape
Where from hour to hour
It may never see a single irksome thing.

Raw beauty is a daily rule of life,
Rather than an elitist exception
Tussled over by investors in art
Who crudely see beauty as the hardest currency there is –
The lifeless prop of nest-building pride.

And perhaps, when that incessant, enrapturing beauty
Lying just beneath the surface, free of any price-tag,
Perennially suffuses your whole being
As you move through a world without boxes, or walls, or doors,
   or roads,
With no one ever between you and the sky,
Leaping through three dimensions towards whatever takes
   your fancy,
You would be different.

And close to,
Drawn into the dolphin's force-field,
Smitten by the shamanistic glimmer
In an eye that distils a life-long exposure
To another, rarer state of things,
You too are alchemically touched –

And when asked what it was like
Will find yourself saying, 'It was beautiful,'
Unselfconscious with the obviousness of the word.

The sun begins to set in the Blasket Sound,
Silhouetting the two sugar-loaf shapes
Of Inishvickillane and Inishnabró,
Their fissures fading in the dusk.

The dolphin rises slowly,
Its head lying above the water,
And closes one eye.
It rests alternate halves of its brain,
Never wholly sleeping,
Like the Awakened One,
The sobriquet of the sleepless Buddha.

A boat appears.
An emerging blur along the coastline from Dunquin.
The dolphin opens both eyes,
Giving the object an evaluating glance.

It whistles softly,
Chirrups,
Opens its blow-hole,
Then half closes it to emit a taut, brief trumpet,
Rasps and clicks.

One sound is repeated,
Slowly seeming more recognisable than the rest:
' . . . Offfeee . . . offfeee . . . '
Not unlike ' . . . dolphin . . . dolphin . . . '
The word that you were shouting earlier,
Uneasily.

It swims towards the boat,

Reappearing at the stern,
Inspecting its propeller circumspectly,

Then leaps high out of the water, above the gunnels,
To glimpse those on board.

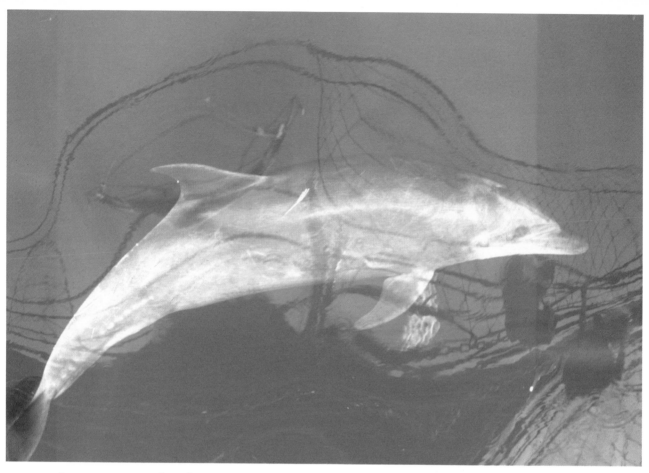

A story runs that its parents were caught and drowned in
    bottom nets
And it connects the sound of an engine with their death,
Allowing no boat to pass without being closely vetted.

The story runs that years ago,
When the two bodies were brought up on deck,
Their skin cut into, griddled by nylon filaments,
Their eyes pecked out by crabs,
A two-foot dolphin followed the trawler into the bay
And wriggled beside it, haunting it for months . . .

The boat approaches.
'You all right so?'
'All right.'
The meagre exchange seems to accentuate the cold.

'You want a spin . . . ? We're going back.'
You clamber aboard,
Your shivering body perfidiously grateful for the ride.
The engine grinds back into gear.

As you gaze wistfully at a plume of incandescent vapour
You hear someone on board drily declare below his breath,
'... Another one quare for the fuckin' dolphin.'
And you catch a reciprocal nod of assent out of the corner of
   your eye,
And an indifferent snort
From his companion.

You are presently asked if you want a blanket
And regarded like some disaster victim.
No longer competent. Out of it. Looked at as though through
   double-glazing.

'Treacherous tides,' someone adds, flatly,
But with enough emphasis to ensure you know you're being
   rescued.
And a look that says he hopes you know enough to buy him a
   drink.

The boat finds its way past the Towérin Bán,
Entering the blind harbour of Daingean Uí Chúis
And its sheltered leaden lagoon.

You stare back at the horizon and the last black fleck
Of that spirit moving upon the face of the waters;

You catch the peripheral comments of the trawlermen.
'He's a big fish altogether.'

'There's a museum that would want him surely.
You'd be several hundred pounds to the good.'
'If you could catch him, you'd be rotten with money.'

'Ah, he'll be flushed out soon enough when the harbour's
    dredged.
That'll interrupt his life for keeps.'

'Yirra Christ, he should be rid of before then.
He does more damage than the fuckin' seals.
You ever seen his teeth? They'd tear your fuckin' tripes out.'
'He takes a ton of fish a day.'

The dolphin has moved towards Valencia,
In the direction of the Atlantic,

At the last glimpse
Still glowing with that selfless zen smile,

Leaving you to a more familiar cold
And the dubious journey home.

But part of you from now on is out there, all at sea.
And you stand in a rain-squall
On the Kerry quayside
As bereft as a fish discarded from the daily catch,
Mouthing on the concrete;

But with something unaccountable added.

To taste.

Picture Credits

The author and publishers are grateful for permission to reproduce the following illustrations: Paul Ashley and Elizabeth Williams (p. 7); Sue Balfe (p. i); Michael Diggin (p. 17); Brian Holmes (pp. ii, 11, 13 *bottom*, 14, 18, 29 *bottom*, 31 *bottom*, 39 *top*, 42 *top*, 43 *top*, 50-1, 53, 57, 71, 72 *top and bottom*, 73 *top*, 81 *top and bottom*, 86 *top and bottom*, 89 *bottom*, 91 *bottom*, cover and 95, 96, 97 *bottom*, 104 *bottom*, 107 *bottom*); Neal D. Jackson (p. 40 *bottom*); Christoph Laschet (p. 9); Tim Lawless (p. 34 *top*); Lars Löfgren (p. 82 *top*); Rico Oldfield (pp. 16 *bottom*, 19, 22, 23, 29 *top*, 37, 66, 68, 76, 87, 92, 97 *top*, 112); Joe Ryle (p. 75); Sheila Stokes (pp. 26, 30 *bottom*, 31 *top*, 33 *top and bottom*, 35 *top and bottom*, 38 *top and bottom*, 54, 55, 56 *top and bottom*, 60, 61, 64 *top*, 67, 77 *bottom*, 89 *top*, 94 *bottom*); John White (pp. 48 *top*, 52, 62, 74 *top*); Chris Williams (pp. 15 *top*, 16 *top*, 24, 25, 28, 34 *bottom*, 39 *bottom*, 43 *bottom*, 59, 64 *bottom*, 94 *top*); Paul Williams (pp. 27, 36); Bernd Würsig (p. 101 *top*); all other photographs by Heathcote Williams.